Entering

The *World*

Of The

Supernatural

Entering

The World

Of The

Supernatural

Where the Supernatural Becomes Natural

Barbara Goddard

XULON PRESS

Xulon Press
2301 Lucien Way #415
Maitland, FL 32751
407.339.4217
www.xulonpress.com

Paperback ISBN-13: 978-1-66285-031-8
Ebook ISBN-13: 978-1-66285-032-5

Vision

All of my life I had a heart for those that are less fortunate than myself. I believe that God has given me a calling to take care of them. I found out where God guides he provides. It breaks my heart to see people sleeping outside especially when it is cold. I saw not only adults but children too that were sleeping in cars. It hurts me to see adults and children eating out of the trash and then I go home and can eat anything I want to eat. I told my husband we have to do something for these people. We started making pans and pans of food. I didn't throw anything together either. I cooked for them as though I was cooking for my family. We made pans of baked chicken, string beans, seasoned rice, and cornbread. They love my food. I made sure that everybody that was out there got a plate. We took plenty of water and drinks. My husband prayed with them and I fed them. Every time we would go feed the homeless the lines would get longer and longer. At first, it was just men but after a while, it was men, women, and children. The people were so nice. They were people just like me and you, they just did not have homes. I got to know a lot of them. I found out that a lot of them had college degrees. A lot of them came to Florida for a better life, but for whatever reason, they are living on the streets now. I didn't even know they had homeless people in Florida. I came to Florida after traveling around the world being in the military. In the military we have everything. We were not around homeless people. I was only told about the good things in Orlando like Disney, Universal Studios, and shopping sprees. Nobody told me about the need that Florida had. Instead of hanging out at Disney and Universal Studios, I began to do the will of God. We started feeding between two hundred and fifty to three hundred men every other Saturday. After feeding them on Saturdays my husband would pray with the men and pass out bibles, and on Sundays, I would pick up the women and children to have bible study in my home with them. We feed them spiritually and naturally. After a while, I told my husband this is too big for us. The group was growing larger and larger. I said I wish I had a home that these children can come to just to have fun. A place where they can relax, play games, ride horses and have counselors just in case they are dealing with depression or suicidal thoughts. Some kids don't understand why they are sleeping in shelters or on the streets. This would be a place where some of them can visit but some would stay and call this home. Every penny I collect from this book will go directly to the children and their needs. This is why I share my testimonies not only to help your faith grow but to bring these innocent little children off the streets. All I need is for that one person to give that donation that will change my life and in return, I will change the lives of children, one child at a time. God bless whoever reads this book. I pray that your faith will soar like an eagle and you too can do all things through Christ that strengthens you... Love your sister in Christ Barbara Goddard.

Table of Contents

Introduction

Maybe you heard about supernatural signs, spiritual encounters, and miracles. You wondered are they really true? I know what the Bible says about it, but can it really happen in my life? Of course, it can now let me explain to you the different experiences I have encountered.

Sometimes you may feel like I am tired of normal church, I really want to see more, I want to see a move of God. You are so hungry for a move of God to the point where you want this Bible that we talk about to come alive, come alive in you.

After you hear my different testimonies in this book, you will realize that God still does miracles. He still moves supernaturally, and you can still have spiritual encounters with the Lord. God will allow anyone to experience these encounters and miracles. You don't have to be saved for fifty years or have a Ph.D. in theology. I didn't do anything special to have these experiences, I am just in love with Jesus.

This book will change your life forever, it is for all religions and skeptics alike. If you are willing to read this book from cover to cover trust me it will take your faith to a whole new level.

My life has been transformed, I was supposed to die, doctors told me in Nov. 1984 that there was nothing else they could do for me but God had other plans for my life. God has not only done miracles in healing for me but in every part of my life. Family, friends, and doctors can testify to all of my testimonies.

The Love Experience

I can recall when I was about nine years old while playing outside with some of my friends, I had a supernatural experience. The curfew was set by my mom, which was I had to be in the house before the streetlights came on. On one particular night, the street lights came on while I was still playing outside. My mom came to the door and reminded me to come in. I said "ok", as I proceeded to climb up the stairs. I can still picture those five steps vividly, which I had to climb. Climbing up the first step, no problem, upon climbing up the second step, it seems as though a pair of hands were wrapped around my waist, which caused me to be frozen in place. Again my mom called for me to come into the house, but I could not move, and I told her "I couldn't move". She said, "you better come into this house", I said, "Mom for real I can't move ". She said, "Then this will help you move". Oh my goodness! She had a belt in her hand. I said, "Mom", and began to cry. When she saw me crying she knew something was wrong. I literally felt invisible arms wrap around my waist. My body was frozen in a walking position, and the only functioning body parts were my eyes and mouth. By this time she was awe-struck and believed me. Knowing something was wrong, she kept staring at me in disarray and amazement. She asks what's wrong. And I answer, "I don't know". I was just baffled as she was. All of a sudden the arms release me, "blurting out mom I can move now". I couldn't wait to go back to my room and ask the Lord what had just taken place outside. Upon entering my room I said, "Lord I was so scared and embarrassed". Somehow I knew God had something to do with that unusual experience that just took place. He proceeds to ask me a series of questions. The Lord said, "Do you remember how you met with me every day, and do you remember our times of fellowship"? I replied, "Yes Lord". "Do you remember writing me letters on a daily basis"? I replied, "yes again". Continuing, he said, "I was there when your sister hurt you by teasing and mocking you, stating the only thing she ever does is write a letter to Lord". "I was there when you were persecuted for my name". I said, "Lord I remember it all". He proceeds to say, "Barbara you have perfected love for me and so I came to take you home with me. However, because I love you and did not want to embarrass you, that's why I took my hands away from your waist". Perfected: make completely free from faults or defaults, or as close to such a condition as possible. Being without defect or blemish. That's how my love was for my Heavenly Father was, and still is today. Later on my Father, God showed me the hands that were wrapped around me. I want to urge everyone that reads this book to please fall in love with Jesus. He's not a fairy tale, and please don't miss the opportunity to worship him, in spirit and truth

2nd Corinthians 12: 1-3 it is doubtless not profitable for me to boast. I will come to visions and revelations of the Lord: I know a man in Christ who fourteen years ago— whether in body I do not know, or whether out of the body I do not know, God knows— such a one was caught up in the third heaven. And I know such a man — whether in the body or out of the body I do not know, God knows—

The Love Experience Continue

One day while in worship, I knew I was standing before the throne of God. The glory of God came to the room and filled the entire place of worship. According to 2nd Chronicles 5:14, *the Glory of God was so thick, it was practically impossible for the priests to minister for the glory of the LORD filled the house of God.* The presence of God was unbelievable, just spectacular. Everyone was involved in worshiping the Lord on that day. The children were crying out to God. His manifested presence was so thick in the sanctuary that all I could remember was, falling down during worship. My husband said he tried to catch me because I fell out instantly, it happened too fast. The power of God knocked me on the tile floor, from a standing position, directly on my back. Like Philip was translated to another place in the spirit I felt the same thing happened to me. I've always tried to be cautious because of a herniated disc in my back. This was a result of an injury that lasted for about five years. Suffering lots of back pain was common during those five years. So I often tried not to be too physical, or radical while worshipping; anyone can understand my cautiousness. Once the glory cloud appears in the service that day, nothing matters anymore to me. I had to be a part of what my Father God was doing, I was told, I fell so hard that the saints thought I had damaged my head or my back, but to my surprise when I got up, I was completely healed of my back injury, My Father God supernaturally healed me. Another miracle of healing took place during that service as well. For about ten years my son Elisha suffered from asthma. Visiting numerous hospitals because of many asthma attacks somehow became normal. Frequent visits to the emergency room became a routine. At times we would visit the hospital on a weekly or biweekly basis which took place for many years. While in service that day, God said "Go tell your son Elisha, I have given him new lungs". He rejoices and blesses the Lord, for the word from the Lord, and the miracle of receiving new lungs that day. After the service was over, my son had another severe asthma attack (or a symptom attack) and was rushed to the Emergency Room. The doctor said," Oh I'm so sorry Elisha, to hear that you had another asthma attack". Elisha responded, "oh no doctor, I don't have asthma", to which I replied, "He doesn't have asthma anymore, these are just symptoms". Nevertheless, the medical professional treated him for asthma, by prescribing asthma medications. The medication was not effective and did not work, because during that night he had another severe attack (or what it seems to be another attack). He came to me, "Mom, I thought you said God gave me new lungs", I said, " you do, Elisha", but "The new lungs don't know how to function properly in your body, you must talk to your new lungs, and command them to work right". Moments later, I heard my son saying, "New Lungs, I'm not supposed to be coughing, and breathing like this, I command you to operate right in the Name of Jesus". Immediately the symptoms stopped and never returned. That miracle really took place in our worship service, over four years ago. Elisha no longer suffers from asthma anymore. During the manifested presence of God's glory, one of the youth said he felt the need to take a picture in front of the church. Why does he feel he should take pictures, well he said God told him to do it (please see the image below) This is the picture of the image we caught on camera, it appears to be a face coming out of the light.

Love Experience
Part III

P lease keep in mind that I cannot list all the supernatural experiences I encountered with Father God,
however, I will attempt to list as many as the Holy Spirit
allows me to share and reveal at this time. One night
while sitting in the living room enjoying Christian music.
Immediately, I felt the urgency to pray, turning the music
off, I proceeded to cry out to Father God. Believe me when
I tell you I didn't try to make anything happen. The spirit
of my Father God fills the room. I can remember this
encounter very vividly. As I began to pray, I felt as though
I was standing in the presence of Father God. The atmosphere changed and his glory filled the room. Do you know
what the feeling is like, When you haven't seen a friend in
a long time, and it is as though you can't wait to tell them
everything? That's how I felt during that episode when
his presence came into the room. Thanking and praising
him was minor compared to what was really going on in
my soul and spirit. Words cannot put into action what
took place in the presence of God. My best description

of that moment can be only described as a vast amount of joy pouring into my soul and spirit. Somewhere in the midst of the encounter, I heard the Lord speaking, " I want to work miracles through your hands, I want you to lay hands on the sick, and they will recover", and he also said, "Barbara I want you to do like I did when I walk the earth". I did not respond with my mouth vocally, but in my spirit, I responded by saying "Yes Lord"

> *John 14:12-13, Most assuredly, I say to you,*
> *he who believes in Me, the works that I do*
> *he will do also; and greater works than these*
> *he will do, because I go to My Father. And*
> *whatever you ask in my name, that I will do,*
> *that the Father may be glorified in the Son.*

I said "Lord I'm available to you," he said, "I want to start using you now. People are dying, I want you to lay hands on them and they will recover". God went on to say "When I walked the earth, I healed all manner of diseases, the epileptics and the paralyzed people". I could actually feel his words pouring into my spirit. " I want to use you in the Supernatural Power of God with signs and wonders". I replied "yes Lord". He also mentioned," if you can, believe me, I will use you, daughter". In return, I said, "Lord I believe you, and you can use me" his response was, "if you can trust me I will". That's exactly what took place during that encounter because he poured out his word and spirit in me, I couldn't wait to be used by him.

Miraculously Testimonies

> Matthew 9:35 Then Jesus went about all the cities and villages, teaching in their synagogues, preaching the gospel of the kingdom, and healing every sickness and every disease among the people.

Two days later, I said to my husband, let's go and be a blessing to my mom, and purchase a suit for her. Upon our arrival at the location, we realized the store moved to another location. After lunch, we arrive at the prescribed location, without finding the dress store. I mentioned to my husband "this is a good day, and let's go home". On the way, we saw a woman walking who appeared to be handi-capped with very limited mobility. Her arms were fixed as though she had endured a stroke, it also appeared she was punching herself in her face because of the positioning of her arm, directly located on the jaw area of her face. May I remind you, she was walking very slowly to a merchant store. When my eyes made contact with her; low and behold the spirit of God rose up in me and immediately I asked my husband to turn around. "Let's go and pray for that lady". I remember what God had spoken to me about walking in the Supernatural". As I approach this complete stranger, strangely as it may seem, it seems as though she was expecting us. Her eyes were directly fixated upon us. Asking her very gently, Ma'am can we pray for you? She responded with a big "Yes". May I remind you that I was still in the vehicle, and I couldn't wait to exit the vehicle. Before my husband could park the vehicle, I jumped out of the car, quickly approached her, with much confidence and a humble spirit. Addressing her, with these words, "ma'am God said that I can lay hands on the sick and they will be healed", she sat on the bench in a waiting position. The temperature was very hot and sunny on that blessed day. While approaching her our eyes were fixated on each other, within a couple of feet away from her my shadow touched her.

> Acts 5:15 Insomuch that they brought forth the sick into the streets, and laid them on beds and couches, that at the least the shadow of Peter passing by might overshadow some of them.

Please allow me to say that again, it wasn't me but my shadow touching her, and immediately, her hand that was fixated on her face dropped. "Hallelujah, look at God! Look at God, did you see that", she exclaimed very excitedly! I said, "All glory goes to God". Then she turns and looks at me, with a question, "Who are you?" I replied, "I'm just someone that wants to be used by God. He's the one that healed you, not me". She was so happy that her hand was no longer stuck in her, she forgot about her fingers were still balled up, it looked as though she was making a fist. I ask her, "Ma'am can you please open your hand"? she replied, "baby I can't open my hand, it has been like this for years", in response to her statement, I said, "In the name of Jesus open your hands" Immediately her fingers started popping open one by one. I said thank you Jesus look at my God. He healed you right in front of Wal-Mart. She said my daughter said that I would be healed but not now. She said, "Mommy God is going to do it but just wait". I told her that *Hebrews 11:1* Says now faith is *the substance of things hoped for and the evidence of things not seen.* I told her God wanted to heal her now and he did just that.

Father God deals with the now, he is a God of the present, not of the past. One day, someday and one of these days are not days listed on the calendar. We do realize that God has appointed times to perform some acts, however when it comes to our healing, and deliverance today is the day of salvation.

The lady and I began to praise God for her miraculously healing. Remember, what I said earlier, describing her walk? She moved at a very slow pace, it appears as though she was taking baby steps. After the encounter with the Holy Spirit, she was now walking very fast. She no longer had to take baby steps as she was praising God. People were looking at her as she was going into the store rejoicing in the Lord. She was saying thank you, Jesus thank you, God. God is good and greatly to be praised. He desires for us to walk in the supernatural arena with signs and wonders.

> ***Mark 16:17*** *And these signs will follow those who believe; In my name, they will cast out demons; they will speak with new tongues;*

All believers are supposed to be operating in the supernatural realm, not just the fivefold ministry.

A Supernatural Angelic Experience

O ne night while all my children were sleeping, this is usually the time that I can have quiet time with God. This is a time of fellowship and communion. If you can recall earlier I mention that I look forward to meeting with Father God, mostly at night every night. My love for my Heavenly Father is so deep, I really can't articulate it in mere words, however, I will tell you this much, some of these experiences are not ordinary and it's beyond anything in the natural realm I can find to compare it to. For a lack of words, all I can say is it's the supernatural realm of God. We can't go in our flesh to commune with him, because he is not a fleshly God. To worship him you must be in the spirit (John 4:24). Now back to my story, as I was folding up clothes and meditating on the lord. All of a sudden I sense that I was not alone. I knew my children and husband were sleeping. The sense of someone else in the room was very strong, turning around, and behold there stood a nine-foot angel standing in my living room. I knew he was nine feet because my ceiling was nine feet and his head touched my ceiling. His exact words were, "I'm sent from heaven to take your prayer request", my response was, "oh my goodness". Frozen in place would be the best way to say how I responded to this angelic visitation. I was so surprised that I did not give a prayer request. I began to thank God for allowing me to have this angelic visitation. I felt that this was an honor because everyone does not see angels. After I experienced this visitation, I began to have lots of angelic visitations. I began to hear the voice of God very clearly. After this encounter, God said, "Barbara you ask angels to guard and protect your house as you sleep", I said, "I sure did", He said, "I command the angels to walk and down in your house, "He also said I found your house to be dwelling place for my glory", I am so honored to hear such powerful words. After he told me this he said, "be careful of the company you entertain, and things that come through the T.V", in other words, we will reverence him even with our house. I got my family all together and told them what the Lord had spoken to me. My children believe in God just like me. They know to keep the house clean at all times, and to watch what comes through the T.V. We really take *2 Corinthians 7:1* seriously.

> *Therefore having these promises, beloved, let us cleanse ourselves from all filthiness of the flesh and spirit, perfecting holiness in the fear of the lord.*

I will not offend the Lord with my actions

Supernatural Healing

At about the age of 16, I had a bleeding disorder, which the doctor did not know what caused it. All I know is the doctors could not find a cure. In *Mark 5:25-34,* there was a lady that had an issue of blood, our stories are so similar but different in that she suffered for 12 years while my bleeding disorder only lasted nine years. For twelve years she went from physician to physician, spending all her money, while remaining in the same condition. My friend, I did the same, from doctor to doctor while remaining in the same condition. At the time I was in the military, I had to still perform my duties, which consisted of working in the office, and I still had to perform my soldierly duties, it was very difficult. How I manage, I cannot say, only it was by the grace of God, I kept trusting and believing that God would heal me. The Bible continues to say that this lady could not lift herself up. She was bent over, and I was the same way. I felt as though if I stood straight up, I would have popped every organ in my body. I was in need of a miracle. The physicians tried everything, at one time I was prescribed up to, 36 pills a day. I was faithful in obeying the doctors' orders, seeking a cure. The medications just made me drowsy and sleepy at all times. The physicians also performed four surgeries attempting to rectify the problem, which did not work. During this time my husband was not stationed with me, and that was a good thing because, in reality, I was not ready to be a wife (or perform my wifely duties). it seems as though the more I kept believing God, the sicker I became, and my situation looked dim. The physician suggested a Removal of my Fallopian tube, this remedy would stop the bleeding. In my desperation, I gladly agree. Sometime after the surgery, we soon found out this didn't work either, because the problem still exists. This experience is so vivid in my mind, it seems like only yesterday. I won't go through the whole story, but I told God that when the Fallopian tube was removed I was young and did not know any better about trusting you. I ask the Lord for another Fallopian tube just like you would ask for a glass of water. I said Lord will give me a creative miracle. I said will you please give me my Fallopian tube back. He did not answer me but later on about a month later I got very sick and was taken to the emergency room. The doctor asks, "What's wrong?" I said, " I'm having a lot of pain in my right side". He said, "What do you think it is?" I said, "Well when I was overseas I got my right Fallopian tube taken out". He said, "Let me do an ultrasound and x-ray". He came back into the room and said, "Well here is the right tube and the left one too". If I had never felt the pain I would have never gone to the hospital. Yes God does do creative miracles. He has done it for me. But still, due to my persisting ailment, my husband was ordered from Germany to spend some time with me. It was good to have him for moral and spiritual support. One night I remember telling my husband "that I was going to revival service", he suggested, and that I should stay at home and rest a little. I responded, "What do I have to lose? The doctor has given up on me, so I'm going to church". Upon arriving at the church, the Man of God said to me, "Daughter you are like a bird on a tree limb and the trunk of the tree is God, if you don't grab hold of the trunk, you are going to die". Immediately I saw myself as that bird, taking hold of that tree. My faith was stirred at the revival meeting that night. The following night I returned to my regular church service, fell on my knees, and began worshiping before the Lord. Crying out to the Lord, "The physician has given up on me" Somehow I could hear the Word of God from the revival service, which burnt in my heart. This pushed me even further in worship and praying at the altar, I felt like I was in another place, it was a vision.

The Scene of the Vision

My best recollection, I was totally out of my natural self and stepped into the supernatural presence of God. While I was in the presence of God. I had entered another realm, the supernatural realm. I was completely out of the natural realm. I felt so light. During this time I felt no pain at all. I saw Jesus Christ, he was tall and his face was so bright. He wore a long white robe, with a gold rope around his waist. I looked up at him as he stood over the altar, it was as though he was above the altar. His feet did not touch the floor. I was no longer praying but worshiping. *Rev 1:13*, This encounter is so clear in my mind, as though it took place yesterday. He looked at me and handed me his robe, the hem of his garment and I took it. On that day I was completely healed from the sickness, I suffered for so many years, like the woman in the Bible who had an issue of blood. I grabbed the hem of his garment and was healed that day. It was exciting, praising God. I remember calling my husband overseas and describing the whole matter of the vision. I can even remember my phone bill totaling about $650 because we did not have unlimited long distances in those days. We were charged for long-distance calling, this was the time during the '80s. Thank God he can heal all manner of diseases and sicknesses.

> *Matthew 4:23 And Jesus went about all Galilee, teaching in their synagogues, and preaching the gospel of the kingdom, and healing all manner of sickness and all manner of diseases among the people.*

So it does not matter what kind of sickness or disease you may be facing, Jesus can heal you of anything that seems impossible. I'm so glad that he healed me because the doctors did not have a cure for my sickness, but Jesus did.

Dream Experience

A llow me to testify a bit, on the goodness of the Lord. I once had a dream about someone I hadn't seen in about eight years. In the dream, I was instructed by God that she needs a miracle. I was also told, I must go and pray for her. Naturally, I respond by stating, "Father, I don't know where she lives, and I knew her very briefly, being that I only met her once a couple of years ago". His response was, "I will make the connection". Humbly offer my obedience, mainly because I have found out that faith produces obedience. *Deuteronomy 5:33,* Just like God told Abraham, I want to make you a great nation, and I'm going to take you to a place where you know nothing about. But you must leave all your familiar surroundings and all of your families and friends behind. When he left home he did not know where was going, but he obeyed God the Father.

Genesis 12:2, And I will make of thee a great nation and I will bless thee, and curse him

> *that curseth thee. And in. thee shall all the*
> *families of the earth be blessed.*

Abraham followed the instructions of the Lord and received his inheritance. Now getting back to me. Remember I hadn't seen this young lady in about eight years, nevertheless, the Lord gave me a word and I had to obey. Through my obedience, the pathway began to brighten and start taking light. One day, one of my friends ran into the lady I'm supposed to pray for, my best friend. Of course, she notifies me. I got so excited I asked her can I please have her friend's phone number. Her friend says let me check, to see what she says, so I patiently waited. My friend told the lady to tell her best friend to please contact me because I have a message for her from the Lord. Please notify your best friend that God has heard her prayers, and I need to speak with her concerning a miracle the Father says she needs. This whole episode took about a month to unravel. When I finally got in touch with the lady that needed the miracle, I asked her, did she remember me. She said, "No can you refresh my memory". I reminded her of an episode when she was brought into a church, due to severe back problems. At the time she couldn't walk and had to be carried to the church altar, the pastor was asked to pray for her, however, I was designated to pray for her. During the prayer session, the supernatural power of God fills the room, and suddenly, she jumps out of the chair, commencing to praise God.

God healed her back problems. Then she recalls the entire episode and me as well. At this time we got focused on the current situation at hand and she asked "what is the message God gave you", I began to tell her about the dream I had about her, and how God said she was in need of a miracle. She responded, by saying, I had a vision, a great light came into the room and the Lord spoke to me and said it was not my time to die. He said I'm going to heal you and give you a miracle. At the same time, she had the vision, I had the dream and she mentions she had cancer throughout her body. With some encouraging words, I respond that there is nothing too hard for God, We are going to obey God, and we will receive your miracle. I proceed to ask her for her address so we can make contact, for me to come and pray for her, she quickly complies. Sometime thereafter we agree to meet. Arriving at her home, I was escorted upstairs by the housekeeper. She was resting in bed discouraged and partially immobilized. Her appearance did not match the sister I once knew, whose appearance was once very vibrant and healthy. she seems somewhat of a shell compared to the lady I once knew, very weak and frail lying in the bed. She had very limited mobility, she could not get out of bed, or use the bathroom without assistance. Looking at her, I still could picture in my mind the lady I once knew eight years ago. Using words of encouragement, I kindly reminded her of the many episodes of how Jesus healed many that were sick and had all forms of diseases *(Matthew 4:23)*. I resume by giving her testimonies after testimonies, pertaining to my healing, which builds her faith. Also, remind her that there was a time when the physicians had given up on me. By this time the room was full of faith, and it was time to pray.

The Prayer Of Faith

> *Is anyone about you sick? Let him call for the elders of the church, and let them pray over him, anointing him with oil in the name of the Lord. And the prayer of faith will save the sick and the Lord will raise him up. And if he has committed sins, he will be forgiven. ~James 5:14-15*

First I start by commanding the Spirit of Cancer, and the Spirit of Infirmity to come out, continuing I command the polluted blood out of her bones and commanded the healthy blood to fill the marrow of her bones and her entire body. Canceling the spirit of death assignment over her life, then speaking the peace of God to flow her body in the name of Jesus. I also command peace to come into her mind. Speaking to every organ that was damaged, to be restored in Jesus' Name. After the prayer, I sang a short song of melodies to her hearing. Immediately, after the song this lady that once lay in the bed immobilized, who needed assistance in every area of her life. Sat up in the bed and said. "I receive my miracle". She said, "That she is getting up to take a shower, and greet her husband upon his arrival home". Remember this was the lady that could not shower without assistance. Expressing our gratitude to the Lord, My husband and I begin to rejoice and bless the name of Jesus, for her healing, and on this joyous occasion, I kiss her goodbye and depart. During our departure the housekeeper asks, "is Natasha asleep?", I responded by stating, "no she's in the bathroom, in the process of taking a shower" to which she responded, "she can't do that on her own" and of course, I responded by stating, "Yes she can, the Lord has risen her up", The housekeeper ran up the stairs immediately to witness the miracle the Lord had performed. I often call to check on her to see how she is doing. She said, "I am walking in my miracle and still believing in God for the impossible". Her body no longer is filled with pain.

Bathroom Experience

One day after Sunday service my family and I went out to dinner. There was another couple that went out to dinner with us that day as well. Once we prayed for our food we began to fellowship and eat dinner. I'm kind of picky with my food and the food wasn't touching my taste buds, so I said, I'm done and went to the bathroom to wash my hands. As I proceeded to go into the bathroom I noticed a lady standing in the bathroom crying. Approaching her, I asked about her wellbeing, to which she replied, "She was okay but a young man almost got her fire from her place of employment". Replying back I said, "Well thank God you still have a job". I could sense and see the sadness in her facial expressions, which she was making. I asked her if she needs prayer, she said please pray for me. While we were in the bathroom, she mentions she was suffering from depression and also had other pains in her body. I told her that Jesus was going to heal her from that depression today right in the bathroom. Praying for her, I said, "I command the spirit of depression to come out of her, right now in the name of Jesus".

I told that foul Spirit of sadness leaves her that she may function the way she is supposed to in her workplace. The spirit of God began to fill the bathroom. Sensing the presence of God. She requested additional prayer for her back and shoulder as well. As we were praying in the bathroom, people began gathering in the bathroom. As people were coming to the bathroom naturally, I would move out of the way, and apologize for being in the way. I kindly said to a young lady to go ahead and use the facilities, she responded by saying "oh no I'm here for prayer", so as I continue on praying another lady came up, again I moved out of the way and apologize but she did the exactly the same thing and requested prayers as well. Quietly, whispering to myself this Is God. He was being lifted up in the bathroom and to my amazement, people were forming a prayer line. All I could say was Lord where did these people come from?

> *John 12:32 And when I'm lifted up from the*
> *earth, I'll draw all men/women to me.*

He did not say he had to be lifted up in a certain place. He (Jesus) said when I'm lifted up, I'll draw men and women to me. Jesus was being lifted up in the bathroom and people were being drawn to him. Living in a hurting world, it's important to lift up the name of Jesus so that people may believe and get saved. Looking at the line, there were people of all races. These women I did not know who they were but one thing I did know, was they needed a touch from the Lord and they got it that day. After the Lord finished using me, one of the ladies I prayed for said, "I want you to know that when you touch my arms something left your hand and traveled through my body, and oh my goodness my shoulder does not hurt anymore". She continues on saying, "I'm a backslidden minister and it's time to come back home" She also said, "In my backsliding state I heard God said he has anointed you this day in the ladies bathroom". Glory to God he is good even in the bathroom.

The Hell Experience

Dream/Encounter ...

Last night I believed I had a dream and the reason I say that like I'm not sure because it was so real. In this dream/encounter, I was telling everybody that Jesus was soon to come back and they needed to repent because I did not want them to go to hell. I was pleading with people. I was saying please give your heart to Jesus, he will come back. The more I pleaded with them the more they ignored me. The dream/encounter shifted and I said I am going to sit down on the sofa. Yes, the sofa was outside. All of a sudden the ground began to shake and I said I better get up because this seems like a sinkhole is over here. When I tried to get up the ground opened up and I was looking down into hell. It was too late and I could not move. The sofa tilted back and I was going into hell with my eyes open. Numbers 16:33 Korah and all his friends and everything he owned were swallowed up when the ground opened up. The sofa flipped upside down and it seemed as though everything was moving in slow motion. I was going down headfirst. I said oh God help me, then I said God when I burn up it will be over. He said, "Remember you will have all your senses in hell". My head went into the fire and I was still talking to the Lord screaming for him to help me. All of a sudden I was sitting in the car trying to explain to my husband what had happened to me. I felt like I was about to lose my mind. My husband called the police for help because he thought I had lost my mind. The police could not do anything so I went back to the streets to witness again. I started pleading with the people again. God told me I had to allow you to experience this so that you know that hell is real. Yes, hell is a real place for those that will not accept Jesus as their personal savior. I continued to witness the coming of Jesus. Everyone still was doing their own thing. I was saying please turn your life to Jesus. It was like I was invisible. Nobody wanted to hear. The Bible tells us to go out and be a witness and compel men to come to Jesus. I was so shaken up by what had happened to me that even though they didn't want to hear about the Lord, I kept saying Lord I don't want to go to hell. The ground began to shake again. When I felt the ground shaking again I said Lord I don't want to go to hell. I said they are not listening but God I can't go to hell. I was crawling on the ground saying Lord I can't and I won't go to hell. While I was crawling on the ground some kind of way I injured my arm. I said Lord this seems so real. He said Barbara, do you remember when you were a little girl and you dreamt about the 5 diamond rings and you woke up looking for the rings and I said yes Lord. He said this is real. He said hell is real. When I woke up the same arm that I injured in my dream/encounter was hurting so bad my husband had to pray and massage my arm. After I woke up I got into prayer. I had to go to the store to pick up some items. My husband said he had to put some air in the tire, I said ok. He said do you have some change I said sure. I reached in my purse to get the change and low behold what comes out the first two rings just like I saw in a dream when I was a little girl. I almost passed out in the car. I said did my daughter put these in my purse. I could not wait to get home so I could ask her. She said no ma'am I don't know where the rings came from. God always does supernatural miracles in my life. I just figure this is another one. If you have not asked Jesus to come into your life, it's not too late to do it now.

Shoe Experience

I served in the military for about eight years and for five of those years I ran in sneakers, which had very little support. I did not use wisdom and while I was actively involved in running during my military career. I did not wear the proper running sneakers, I chose cute sneakers, pretty white sneakers with very little support. Because of the lack of support, I developed tendinitis, therefore I could no longer wear high heels shoes anymore. Suffering from tendinitis involves pain in the ankles area and swelling. Elevating my feet daily, soon became a home remedy, which was supposed to relieve the swelling, and it did not work. I took all kinds of medication to relieve the pain and still, nothing worked. One dawn on me, in the atmosphere of faith miracles take place. Soon I began to feed my faith, feeding upon the word of God became my daily bread. Then in prayer, I said to the Lord, "You saith faith comes by hearing the word of God, Which means hearing it in my inner man, concerning what the Word says about healing.

Psalms 30:2 O Lord my God, I cried to you and you have healed me.

Psalms 107:20 He sent his word and heals them and rescue them from the pit and destruction.

I Just began to feed my faith every day with the word. (In other words, till it overflows). I place in my heart the latter part of this scripture must be fulfilled in my heart. My health was not good, I was in constant pain, sometimes I felt as though the devil was stealing my health and destroying my bones. I didn't see the abundant life in my body. The Lord said, "Barbara bring your ankle in my presence and place them on the altar". When God speaks to me, I obey, and whatever I hear I do. I saw myself going to the altar and placing my ankles on the altar. When I got out of prayer, my ankles were completely healed. The swelling went down, and all aches and pain is gone totally forever amen. Now I can drive my car without my ankles being swollen. All pain is gone and I'm back in my heels again, who wouldn't serve a God like that. All glory goes to God. I can now walk correctly, I can once again wear my high heels. Once I thought this impossible, but thanks be to God who causes me to triumph, I'm healed. I could not wait to go shoe shopping again, glory to God, he healed me. I went to the store and blessed myself with many pairs of shoes, buying a pair of high heel shoes on a weekly basis, this is what I call living life more abundantly. Before I end the shoe experience I would like to share another testimony that I have about how God blessed another lady that I met at the shoe store. While waiting patiently shopping at the shoe store. I notice a sweet little lady trying on a pair of shoes. Lending my opinion on her choice of shoes, "ma'am those are some beautiful shoes" she responds, "I use to wear high heel shoes but no longer because I have tendinitis in my ankles" responding in faith I ask "her who told you that" somewhat startling, she looks up at me, and declared she was a believer in Jesus. Sharing my testimony, right in the shoe store I ask her if she would like a prayer. Of course, she agrees. So I gently prayed with her very quietly, I told her I'm taking your ankles to the altar, in the presence of God. Yes, we were in the store, but in the presence of God. After the prayer, the little old lady picked up the shoes she intended on purchasing. Tired them on, all the pain. was gone. She said oh my goodness I have on heels and they feel mighty. I said to her, those shoes are on me, be blessed in Jesus name. She was so happy God healed her in the shoe store. Thank you, Jesus

The Greatest Grateful Experience

I was just sitting here thinking about the goodness of the Lord. I am so grateful and blessed on today I don't know how to act. I said Lord I should have been dead since November 1984 when the doctor told me that I was going to die and there was nothing else they could do for me. Thank you Jesus I'm still here praising his name my God is awesome. I remember when times were so tough for my family and I felt like I was about to beg, I remembered in the word of God

> Psalms 37:25" I've been young and now I'm old; yet have I not seen the righteous forsaken, nor his seed begging bread".

God would not allow my family to beg, thank you, Jesus. I remember when the doctors said I could not have any children but God said yes you will. I thank God that he blessed me to have two amazing kids. I remember when my husband was laid off from his job so we had to stretch our finances. I said we can't shop the way we want to. I was telling God what I wanted from the grocery store but at that time I did not have the money. I said Lord I thank you for what we have. I had no complaints, just a thank you. We were sitting down watching TV and there was a knock at the door. We looked out of the peephole in the door and saw no one. We opened the door anyway and there were so many bags of food in front of the door. Everything on the list that I wanted was at my door. God is soooo good. I just wanted to give him some praise today. God is good, think of his goodness, and share with me what you are grateful for.

Mark 9:23

First I want to say to anyone that has read my testimonies, I want you to know that miracles don't come because of who you are but by believing in the supernatural. It comes because the Bible says in

> *Mark 9:23 Jesus said unto him, if thou canst believe all things are possible to him who believes.*

When you believe that with God that all things are possible, then you are the believer that will receive and see miracles. Jesus said, if we can believe, then we can receive. Everybody cannot receive, because everyone doesn't believe. When we believe, God gives us an open heaven, meaning we have open doors ready available to us. A person that doesn't believe has a closed mind, which also means, he has closed heaven and closed doors. Seeing someone who is always walking in blessings and seems to have an open heaven in their lives, please don't get angry or jealous, or make bad comments about them.

That person is walking and living in *Mark 9:23*. The Bible says in *3 John verse 2, Beloved I wish above all things that thou mayest prosper and be in good health even as thy soul prospereth.* God doesn't want us just to be saved. He wants us to be blessed, we shouldn't be living in poverty, begging for bread. He doesn't want us living in despair, he wants us to live a victorious life. The Bible says in *John 10:10 The thief cometh not, but for to steal, and kill, and to destroy: I am come that they might have life and that they might have it more abundantly.* Let's begin to walk in the abundant life that God has planned for us to walk in. All things are possible if we can believe.

Faith Experience

I just want to talk about faith for a minute. The Bible says in *Romans 10:17 Behold, his soul which is lifted up is not upright but the just shall live by his faith. The scripture says the just shall live by his faith.*

It's not always easy to live by faith but it can be done, I'm doing it right now. It's easy to say you are living by faith when your bank account looks good, your children are well behaved and you don't have one car but you have about two or three in the driveway. Cabinets are full of food and cars are full of gas. You can go and buy whatever you want when you want to. I often hear people say God is all I need but what happens when he is all you got. How would you feel if you had no car or house to live in? What would happen if you could not feed your children or give them the basic things in life? What would you do if you had no money and no job? Would you quote or would you even believe *Habakkuk 2:4?* The Bible says faith comes by hearing the word of God.

> *Romans 10: 17 so then faith comes by*
> *hearing his word. I often tell people it is easy*
> *to quote the word of God*

But it is totally different to live the word of God. I was without a car before, I was also without a place that I could call home. My bank account was empty and my gas tank. I remember Lord help us, I never cursed or blamed God. I still stood on the word of God. Doctors told me I was going to die in Nov 1984 I still stood on the word. I kept standing even when it felt like I was losing and not winning. Our problem is we will stand when everything is ok. We must stand even when things are not ok. From this day forth let us live by the faith we do earnestly talk about.

> *Hebrews 11:6 But without faith it is impos-*
> *sible to please him: for he that cometh to*
> *God must believe that he is and that he is*
> *a rewarder of them that diligently seek him.*

The Hype Experience

I am so excited about Jesus this morning I just can't really put it in words how I really feel about him. He has been so good to me, even when sometimes I feel I don't deserve it. I thought about the three Hebrew boys, Shadrach, Meshach, and Abednego. These young men were told to bow down and worship the golden image that was set up by King Nebuchadnezzar. When all the music and instruments began to play they kept standing. They were reported to the king, but that did not make them bow down. The king said I just want to know you guys really are not going to bow after I said you had to. The Hebrew boys said that is true. I know the king's blood was boiling hot. To make a long story short the king said you guys are about to be fried. They said not only will we not serve your gods but we will not bow to your golden image. The king was so mad he called for the strongest mighty men to bind them and throw them in the fire. The Bible doesn't say that they walked in the fire freely because who really wants to be burned alive. If the king only knew that throwing them in the fire would have placed them right in the presence of the son of God, he would have never done that. Think about the different situations you have been through and the devil told you that you never accomplish anything in life. Yes, and you stood on the word of God. The devil wanted me to compromise my faith so many times but I refused to do it. He threw everything he had at me, I almost died, lost my home, my husband lost his job. We lost our car. When it seemed as though it could not get any worse, I got pregnant and lost my baby. That was so hard for me but guess what, even though I lost all of that I did not lose my faith in Jesus Christ. Remember the devil can't do anything to us unless God allows him to do it. Life was hard at times, but if the devil only knew that by me losing all that stuff it caused me to fall on my face and worship. It caused me to fall in love with Jesus all over again. If the devil only knew the nights I stayed up and cried all night and was in sooooo much pain, I would get up and say Lord I love you more today than yesterday. It wasn't easy but it was worth it. God is still proving himself to me every day.

> *He is my healer, my provider, my doctor, he is my everything. This is why I am sooooo hyped living for him*

The Big God Experience

G od is bigger and greater than any problem that we can ever have. He can do what no other god can do. I have learned in this life to think big because we serve a great big God. I remember when I was a little girl even till now I would believe God for anything because I just believed and still do believe that he can do anything. He keeps proving himself to me every day. I remember when I was stationed in Wurzburg Germany, one day I got very sick. I was rushed to the hospital. The doctor asked me what was wrong and I said I am having very bad pain in my stomach. They said let's do an ultrasound to see what's going on. They took all kinds of blood work. After all the results came in they told me I had a bleeding disorder in my stomach and that I was bleeding on the inside and I needed emergency surgery, I was scared and very nervous but one thing that I knew was I served a great big God. I served a God that could do anything but fail. I knew he could fix it but how I was still young in the Lord. I had faith but I really didn't know how to operate in it. I thought that all I had to do was believe that the bleeding would stop and it would go away. We must take the word of God and apply it to our lives in faith believing that God would honor his word. I did not know so I had to call my mom for help. I wanted my mom to come overseas to be with me but she was scared to fly. All I knew if I got a chance to talk to my mom she would tell me what to do and everything would be fine. I told the doctor before I get the surgery I need to make a phone call to my mom and he said no. He said you can't make a phone call you must get prep for surgery. One thing about the military it is all about taking orders and he said I command you to get back in your room to prepare for surgery. This was the first time in my life that I did not follow an order. I called my mom and told her what was going on and she said let me call Sister Smith. Sister Smith was a little old lady that prays for people and God always answered her prayers. She got on the phone with me and began to pray, she prayed until I saw myself healed. I was so fired up when I hung up the phone, my faith connected with her faith, and all of a sudden I was no longer scared or nervous. She said God said that the bleeding has stopped and when the doctors examine you again you will see. She said you don't have to get the surgery if you don't want it either. I was very shy at this time in my life, so I did not tell the doctors I did not want the surgery. So I got prep for surgery. Yes, I did, I'll blame it on I was only 18 (laughing). After surgery, the doctor told me that the surgery went well and the bleeding that they saw on the ultrasound was not found in my stomach. Thank God for taking care of that big problem. We serve a big God that loves and cares about every fiber in our body. I thank God I am able to serve him. It is an honor to serve him.

> *The scripture says "but he was wounded for our transgressions, he was bruised for our iniquities; The chastisement for our peace was upon him, and by his stripes, we are healed".*

With the stripes of Jesus, I was already healed. I need whoever is reading this blog to always know that God can do anything that seems so impossible. Remember there is no problem too big that my big God can't handle.

The Back Experience

L et's start out with a question, have you ever been to church and the spirit of God was thick in the building that you didn't know whether you wanted to stand, sit or lay down in his presence?

> *2nd Chronicles 5:13 says It came even to pass, that the trumpeters and singers were as one, to make one sound to be heard in praising and thanking the Lord; and when they lifted up their voice with the trumpets and cymbals and instruments of musick and praising the Lord, saying, for he is good; his mercy endureth for ever: that then the house was filled with a cloud even the house of the Lord";*

It's something about being on one accord. Everybody comes with the same mindset to come and worship the true and living God. We tell God on the way to worship, LORD It's for you I live and for you, I die. We see ourselves by faith in the throne room of God just worshiping him. All we want to do is get into the presence of the Lord. In his presence, nothing else matters just you and him. When you read down to the 14th verse it talks about the glory cloud had filled the place to the point that the ministers could not minister. One Sunday I came to church and in my mind I said Lord it's me and you today, nothing else matters. When the service started you didn't have to tell anyone to worship the Lord, the whole congregation was ready for worship, we were going to meet God. We were all on one accord. We were hungry for a move of GOD. The atmosphere was so thick with his glory, it was as though if we wanted to touch the glory we could. One of the teenagers that were in service that day said he felt as though he needed to start taking pictures, he said he just started snapping the camera. With all that glory that was in the room, I knew something was going to be caught on the camera. When we began to look at the pictures he caught an image on camera. When you look at it, it looks like a face. You can see a nose, mouth, and eyes.

The Supernatural Food Experience

I just wanted to share my supernatural food experience. God is soooooo awesome. I remember reading in the word of God about the two fishes and five loaves of bread that we're able to feed about five thousand men. Jesus told the disciples that the crowd was following him for a while. He knew that they were hungry because they hadn't eaten any food. He knew if he sent them back to their houses they probably wouldn't make it because some of them lived pretty far away. Jesus told the disciples to check and see how much food they had left. They said do you want us to go buy some? They said we can buy at least two hundred worth of denarii and give it to them. Even if they would have bought five hundred worth of denarii it would not have been enough. Jesus said give me what you have, they gave the fish and bread to Jesus. He took that fish and bread and looked up to the heavens and blessed it. He said now set them down because it's time to eat. When God speaks a blessing on or over anything it can't do anything but multiply and prosper. After they ate and were full, they still had food leftover. What a mighty God we serve.

> *The Bible says in the book of John 14:12 "Verily verily I say unto you, He that belie-veth on me, the works that I do shall he do also; and greater than these shall he do; because I go to my father.*

My husband and I did a greater than these experiences. We usually would go out and feed the homeless before the pandemic started. We would pack our SUV up with so much food and drinks. We would usually feed about two hundred men, but this time when we got there we had about three hundred men plus women and children. The first thing I said was Lord please don't let us run out of food. My husband prayed and I said Lord thank you in advance for not allowing us to run out of food. We started feeding the people and I was looking at the food. The food was leaving and the line was getting longer. I kept saying Lord I thank you. All of a sudden it seemed as though it was one man left in line. I said Lord thank you we can feed him. As soon as I said that another person got in line. I said I am so sorry all we have in the bottom of the pot were crumbs left. The young man looked at me and said I will eat the crumbs. That really broke my heart. When I went to pull the crumbs out of the bottom of the pot a whole spoon full of food came out. I said thank you, Jesus.

That day we served chicken seasoned rice, vegetables, and cornbread. After we fed him about 20 more people got in line. We fed that twenty and then after that about another twenty got in line. He kept on providing food so that the people could eat. He would not allow them to eat crumbs. We serve an awesome God. God kept allowing the food to multiply. After everybody was full we still had food and drinks left. The Bible says the just shall live by faith and not by sight. We are not supposed to trust God with our natural eyes but with and through the eyes of God shall we trust him.

> *Romans 10:17 says so then faith comes by hearing, and by hearing the word of God. Come on let's do some greater works than these miracles.*

The Flowers Experience

Now, this is an awesome testimony I would like to share. I remember when we were stationed in Kentucky living in military housing at the time. When we moved into the house every house around us had a beautiful garden. I said to my husband we have to fix our yard up too. We went to the store to get some seeds to plant and every time we planted seeds they never grew. We did everything correctly making sure before we put seeds in the ground it was good. I said why are these flowers not growing. I went back to the store and bought some plant food that still didn't work. We thought maybe it needed more water so we put the sprinkler on it so it can water for a few hours. The water and the plant food still didn't work. We tried everything and nothing worked. I said we need to speak the word of God over this garden.

> *Psalms 1:1-3 says blessed is the man that walks not in the counsel of the wicked, nor stands in the way of the sinners, nor sit in the seat of the scoffers, but his delight is in*

the law of the Lord, and on his law, he medi-
tates day and night. He is like a tree planted
by streams of water that yields its fruits in
its season, and its leaf does not wither. In all
that he does, he prospers.

I said Lord now you said that I am blessed because I do not walk a certain way or sit in certain chairs. You said I am like a tree planted by the streams of water and not only that you said whatever I touch is supposed to prosper and from what I am seeing nothing is happening. I said Lord cause these flowers to grow in Jesus name. Make your name known in my garden. We began to plant seeds again and supernaturally we began to see little buds coming out of the ground. The next thing we knew the flowers were growing like crazy. They were growing so fast we had to constantly clip them because growing out of the garden getting all on the sidewalk. We spoke to our garden and it listened. I believe everything has ears, even the garden. After that, I have been talking to my car, washing machine, tv, and anything that breaks down in my house "laughing ". When it was time for us to leave and go overseas we had to take the garden up and get the house looking the way it did before we moved in for the next family. We got the house all fixed up, and now it was time to work on taking the garden up. We pulled up all the plants in our garden and low and behold two days later they were back again. Yes, fully grown flowers.

My husband pulled them up again and once again they came back. I told my husband if they don't die we will not pass inspection. One minute we were speaking life now we are saying we got to get rid of these flowers. I told my husband when you pull the flowers up this time make an appointment for inspection. He made the inspection for the next day and we passed the inspection. Guess what, they grew back again. While we were processing out we decided to go back and visit the new people that moved into the house, we wanted to really check on the garden. We saw the neighbors standing at the door, we told her who we were and the real reason why we were there. They said we love the house and the neighborhood is beautiful but we can't get rid of these flowers. They just keep growing and growing, we can't get rid of these flowers. I said wow God is awesome. When God puts his hand on something it explodes. We prayed for them to grow now its time to pray and command them to leave.

The New Mindset Experience

I wanted to share a conversation that I had with my nephew last week. He said guess what auntie I am changing my whole house around, instantly in my spirit I said I'm changing my whole mindset around. I knew if I changed my mind my heart and everything about me was about to change.

> Philippians2:5 says "Let this mind be in you, which was in Christ Jesus.

In order to change our mindset to be like "*whatsoever things are of good report; if there be any virtue, and if there be any praise, think on these things*". In order for Jesus Christ to please his father, his mind had to be pure just like his father. Even though he came in the form of a man, he still did not make provisions for the flesh. Jesus set a perfect example for us letting us know that we could do the same thing. They beat him, they lied on him, they spit on him, they put a crown on his head that dug down into his flesh and he did not say a mumbling word. He was constantly criticized because of the assignment he had on his life. How many times did someone beat us because of our stand for Christ, or put nails in our hands or feet?

The average Christian today all someone has to do to us is look at us the wrong way. We forget about what's pure, just, honest, and of a good report. We must have the mind of Christ. When we have a new mindset we must watch what we say and do.

> John 4:34 Jesus said to them, My food is to do the will of him who sent me and to finish his work.

Did you hear what he said, he said his food is the very thing that gives us strength daily. In other words, he is saying I don't care about anything but to do the will of my father. In order for us to be like Jesus, we must change our mindset to be like Jesus. We must watch the words that come out of our mouths because I found out that words are powerful. This world was formed by words. *Proverbs 18:21* puts it this way: *The tongue has the power of life and death.* The stakes are high. Your words can either speak life, or you can speak death. Our tongues can build others up, or they can tear them down. KJV says *Death and life are in the power of the tongue: and they that love it shall eat the fruit thereof.* The best thing we could ever do in this lifetime is to fall in love with Jesus all over again. We can change our world and mindset by speaking positive words.

The Covid-19 Experience

A couple of months ago I had the privilege of experiencing Covid-19. Let me take a moment to let you know it was not a pretty picture either. Every part of my body was in pain. I couldn't eat or drink for three weeks, my mouth was so dry when I would brush my teeth and wash my mouth out my tongue felt like wood. The doctor said as long as you can breathe stay hydrated and treat it like a cold. I believe I had every symptom COVID-19 had to offer. I was in sooooo much pain one day. I told my husband to call different people to pray for me. Every person he called did not answer the phone. I said don't worry about it we will pray together. The pain was so intense I said babe you must pray harder, I just wanted the pain to stop. I began to pray for myself. I prayed until I knew heaven was open. I prayed until all of a sudden I was in the throne room of God. It was so beautiful. I no longer felt pain anymore. While I was having my experience with God I saw a table there. I told God how I felt and that I needed him. I saw God standing behind the table. I said God I am going to get up on the table because I need you. I heard him say Barbara, and yes I heard him call my name. He said if you get on this table I will cover you. I climbed onto the table and curled up like a little baby. I believe I took this position because now I am with my father and he is going to take care of me. I laid there and he covered me up. When he covered me up I fell asleep in his presence. When I came to myself it was about four hours later. That was the best sleep I had in three weeks. When I got up I was totally healed. I was able to drink and eat. I came downstairs for the first time in three weeks. My kids were so happy as though I was just returning from a vacation. I thank God that I am alive. So many people died from COVID-19. Through the whole Covid experience I still trusted my God. We must pray for those who lost their love ones that God would just hold them during this time. My advice to you no matter what problem you may encounter please get in the presence of the Lord and watch him fix it for you. He is able to do more than we can ever imagine.

Memory Lane Experience

I just want to start off by saying I serve a great God. To know him is to love him. My husband and I were watching a funeral of a police officer today. We did not know this officer but we wanted to hear the young lady that was about to sing at the funeral. The song she did was when you hear of my home going don't worry about me I'm just another soldier gone on home. When I heard this song it reminded me of my childhood days. I used to love this song as a little girl. It was sad but I liked it a lot. This song reminded me of when I would sit and write letters to God every day. I did not grow up in a lavish lifestyle. My mom worked two jobs, my father worked for the gas company and made good money but he was an alcoholic. He said he wanted to stop but could not. I remember living in a gang-infested neighborhood where there was killing on a daily basis. People on drugs and selling drugs as well. I believe God allowed me to see how he kept me safe in the middle of all of that. Even though all of that was happening all I wanted was to be in the presence of the Lord. After I got out of school every day I could not wait to meet God with my tea and toast. I wanted to go to church all the time but my mom only went on Sundays. I met a minister from church who used to go to church during the week so I asked him can I start going with him and he said yes. It was going really well until he asked me for a kiss and I was about twelve years old. Here I am falling in love with Jesus and the devil sent this so-called minister into my life, thank God that he was not able to take advantage of me God kept me safe again. He kept me throughout the years and is still keeping me, oh how I love him so much. I thank God for how I grew up with a mom that worked all the time and did not have time to spend quality time with us. I thank God for a dad who was in and out and when he was in he was drunk. All of the things that took place in my life are a testimony today. I know how to raise children even though I was was not taught how. My husband loves God as much as I do so he doesn't do anything that would cause hurt and danger to his family. My dad gave his life to the Lord before he died. thank you, Jesus. My mom is still here at the age of eighty-eight totally sold out to God. Sometimes parents don't have a clue about training their children, such behavior should be natural. Nevertheless I have forgiven them. I just thank God that Jesus came into my life and saved me. I said all of that to say this no matter what you go through or are going through, remember

this is a testimony for someone else just ask ᴄ
peace as you go through different situations.

> Jeremiah 29:11 says (For I know the
> thoughts I think towards you, says the
> Lord, thoughts of peace and not of evil,
> to give you a future and a hope).

Creative Miracle Experience

The Bible says for we walk by faith and not by sight. Before I gave my life to the Lord I believed I loved him so much because I would always find a corner in my house to have conversations with him. I would write letters to the Lord all the time. I remember writing the name Jesus all over the paper. I remember my sister saying she is crazy writing letters to Jesus and writing his name all over the paper. I was just so in love with him maybe because I did not have a father in the home. God was a father to me and I felt as though I was his daughter.

God taught me from a little girl how to be respectful and how to love my neighbor. He taught me how to trust him and not to worry about anything. I would say that I loved him with my whole heart, but that wasn't true because I had not accepted him as my personal savior. I prayed every day, read the word of God every day, and wrote him daily but yet I did not know him. I knew him in my mind and from my lips but my heart was so far from him. To tell the truth, no one ever taught me how. I don't even remember them having altered calls at my church. I remember when I turned sixteen I enlisted in the United States Army, and that was the day my aunt asked me if I had given my life to the Lord. I told her everything that I was doing and she said that is good but not good enough. She said you must accept Jesus Christ as your savior.

I asked her how do I do that and she walked me through the process and I gave my heart to the Lord. In saying that I ask whoever reads this book, don't just take your children to church tell them about Jesus, and have an alter call in your house, you don't have to wait until Sunday. When I accepted Christ in my life that's when everything really began to open up for me. I was in love with him but spiritually I was blind, I wrote letters blindly. I had conversations with him with no sight. But oh my goodness, now that the lights are on, I can really see. My first duty station was Augsburg Germany.

I got really sick over there but guess what the lights were on to my faith. I had to get one of my Fallopian tubes removed. I was so sad because I did not have any children yet. The doctor told me because of the other problems that I have, I will not be able to have children. I said Lord you did not come into my life that I may receive such bad news. I felt the same trust that I felt as a little girl assuring me that everything would be alright. I said Lord I need a creative miracle. I said Lord I want my Fallopian tube back. This was my prayer and I left it like that. I finished my time in Germany and headed back to the states. I said that I would take a thirty-day leave before going to my next duty station. While on leave I got sick and was rushed to the ER. The doctor asked me what was wrong, I remember saying I'm having pain in my right side. He asked me what did I eat, did I fall.

I said it's probably because in Germany I got my right Fallopian tube taken out. He said I will do an ultrasound and x-ray. I said okay thank you. He did what he said he would do. When he came back he said which Fallopian tube was taken, I said the right one. He said are you sure. I said well maybe it could have been the left one (laughing) I knew they took one of them. He said I want you to look at this x-ray. He said here is your right Fallopian tube and here is your left Fallopian tube. I said thank you, Jesus, he gave me a creative miracle. When I said thank you Jesus all the pain left. He had to allow the hurt so that I could see what he had done for me. He is a God that gives body parts thank you, Jesus. If you need anything trust God at his word.

The Worship Experience

I just have to share the greatest worship experience ever. I was sitting in my loft trying to put my foster baby to sleep. She kept crying and trying to get off the chair. If I turn worship music on it actually calms her down. I did not want to turn on my sound system so I said I would do worship myself. I turned off the lights and began to worship the Lord. The more I sang unto the Lord the calmer she became. The room was pitch black so I had to turn on the phone light to see if she fell asleep. I looked at her she was fast asleep. I said thank you Jesus and continue worshiping the Lord. I closed my eyes bowed my head. I began to worship the Lord as though this would be my last time worshiping. When I opened my eyes about an hour later the whole room was lit up. I thought someone had turned on the lights. I could see everything in the loft.

> *2nd Chronicles 5:14 says the priest could not stand to minister by reason of the cloud for the glory of the Lord had filled the house of God.*

I did not see a cloud but his glory was there in the loft. I kept saying Lord fill this place with your glory, he did just that. I want to ask you when was the last time you just let go and let God take over. It's nothing like being in the presence of our savior

The Power Of God Experience

I remember one day when I was stationed in Ft. Knox Kentucky, I had a speaking engagement. The church was called the Hour of Prayer, it was an awesome church. The people were very friendly, it was more like a big family. I was told I had to speak on the power of God. I believe I studied every scripture on the power of God. I said Lord I want this service to be different. I want you to show up and manifest your power in the midst of your people. 2nd Chronicles 5:13-14 says (Indeed it came to pass when the trumpeters and singers were as one to make one sound to be heard in praising and thanking the Lord, and when they lifted up their voice with the trumpets cymbals and instruments of music and praised the Lord saying :) For he is good, For his mercy endures forever. That the house, the house of the Lord, was filled with a cloud, so that the priest could not continue ministering; because of the cloud; for the glory of the Lord had filled the house of God. In order for the glory to fill the house, somebody had to be praying in the house. We can't just go to a church and expect something to happen.

We kick every demonic force that came into the house so they won't hang around and disrupt the service. As I was preparing myself I not only was praying that God would use me, I was canceling the assignment over that house. I remember praying, studying, and crying out to God. I prayed so much I would fall asleep on my knees, and then I wake up and start praying again. I would get in my word and then meditate on the word, and I would keep saying Lord manifest your power in that service. Let your glory be revealed. I would fall asleep studying and then get up and start studying again. When I would wake up I would say the very power of God over and over again. The power was in my spirit. I would even say the power of God was in my bones. I was so excited about the power and all of a sudden I had an allergy attack, you can say it was a demonic attack. I didn't even know I had allergies. This attack from hell tried to blind me. My right eye was on fire. My eye was burning soooo bad but I kept saying the very power of God. I believe I cried all night long. My husband was overseas at the time, and at this time I didn't have children so I was home alone. I said Lord help me, please. All of a sudden I heard the doorbell ring. It was one of the sisters from the church, she wanted to take me shopping to buy a suit. I said I can't see I need to go to the hospital and I can't drive. My friend rushed me to the ER. They said this is a very bad allergy attack. They put something in my eye and I was like thank you Jesus, whatever they used it worked. The doctor said now I have to put a patch over your eye, I said a patch. The doctor said no sunlight can touch this eye. I said ok doctor do what is needed. I said to myself here I am talking about the power of God and I have a patch, nevertheless, I did not lose my focus. When Sunday came I was ready but I was so tired from praying and studying. I said Lord let your power fill the place of worship. When I walked into the building, the Spirit of God was already moving, worship was awesome. When they told me it was time for me to speak, all I said was (The very power of God), that's all I was able to say. The spirit of God came into the room like a mighty rushing wind. The only way I can explain it, was like like God Almighty came into the room in power and glory. Words cannot put into action what took place that day! They were slain in the spirit, drunk in the spirit, and delivered by the spirit of God. People were healed and filled with the spirit of God. The spirit of God filled that place with his glory to the point I didn't have to minister. I knew that the allergy attack I had in my eye never happened again. Glory to God I kept moving bad eye and all. I said that to say this, sometimes God will tell you to do something, and that devil knows if you walk in obedience glory is going to show up. He will send every distraction that he thinks may work on you to abort the assignment but you must keep moving even when it hurts. God bless everyone that read this testimony, may it encourage you to be steadfast in the works of the Lord.

The Arthritis Experience

Now, this experience blew my mind. My husband and I used to go the different nursing homes and pray for the elderly people there. Every visit, our mannerism would to ask for patients who received less or not visitors. The first lady we saw appeared to be about eighty or ninety years old. She was in her room singing old hymns that she sang in her younger days at church. We entered the room and said how are you doing. I am doing fine, she said I was sitting here thinking. She said I served my church for at least seventy years and no one, not even the pastor visited me. I said I am so sorry to hear that but God is good he sent my husband and I just to say that we love you. She was so happy just to have a visitor. As we were walking out of her room we saw a lady sitting in the hallway. She looked so sad so I said can I pray for you. She said I guess so, many people had prayed for me but nothing happened. I said what would you like me me to pray for? She stretched out her arms and her hands were turned inside out. All of her fingers looked as though they were twisted and broken. She said do you still want to pray? I said yes. I told her John 14:12 says Verily verily, I say unto you, He that believes in Me, the works that I do he shall do also, and greater works than these shall he do; because I go to my father. After that, I said now let's pray I spoke healing over her hands, and guess what nothing happened. I was fine with that because I knew God heard my prayer and I knew he was going to allow his power to not only fix her bones but bring her out of the state of depression. She looked at me and said I told you it wouldn't work. I told her I love her, be encouraged and then I moved on to the next person. You must believe what you say when you pray then you can have it. After praying and visiting it was time to go. We told everyone goodbye. The lady that had the severe case of arthritis looked at me like I told you it wouldn't work. I could not listen to that. I told her to continue to pray and trust God. We left and came back about a week later. When we walked in the door this lady came running up to me saying do remember me, I said not really but hello anyway. She said you prayed for me last week. I said I prayed for a lot of people. Of course, I said that to myself. She said I was the one in the wheelchair and my hands were turned inside out. I said oh my God thank you Jesus greater shall we do. I prayed for her hands I didn't even pray for her to get out of the wheelchair. She was so happy running and laughing, no longer depressed. God healed her so good I didn't even know who she was until she told me. I prayed for the arthritis in her hands and God healed her legs too. Don't ever be moved by what see when you are praying. You must be moved by the word of God that says in Mark 11:23 says For verily I say unto you, that whoever shall say unto this mountain, Be thou removed and be thou cast into the sea; and shall not doubt in his heart but shall believe those things which he saith shall come to pass; he shall have whatever he saith. I spoke the word and I believed it and she was totally healed. Praise my God for he is good and worthy to be praised.

The Bragging Experience

Heeeeey I just wanted to brag on my God for a minute. My God is so awesome I can't explain how good he is, but I can explain how good he has been to me. He has opened so many doors to be a witness for him. God has also closed many doors for me too. Yes God does close doors too. Everything that looks good is not God and everything that is of God sometimes doesn't look good, so at the end of the day, he knows what's good for us. Nevertheless, I remembered a time when I used to be so sick and it seemed as though I could not get well. I used to lay in bed and say to God if I had the strength I would run around this room and give you the praise that you deserve. I said Lord while I lay I will not complain but I will think on your goodness. I said Lord, this will be a testimony. I am already healed and manifestation is on the way. While I was waiting on the manifestation of my healing the doctors gave up on me. Guess what I kept believing in God and now here I stand totally healed and set free. How do I know that he is a healer because he healed me. I know him as a provider of finances because when I needed financial help he was there. He provided supernatural money. When I say supernatural money I mean money appearing in my purse $300 dollars at a time in twenties that is. When I would spend that three hundred another three hundred would show up in my purse. Wow God is awesome, isn't he? I remembered one time I was on the way to the store and I told my niece to check my purse to see how much was in my purse. She said it was one twenty-dollar bill, I said ok I said let's go into the store. I planned on using my debit card. I knew I needed more than twenty dollars. After I finished shopping my stuff came up to about one hundred eighty dollars. I reached in my purse to get my debit card and low behold there was another three hundred dollars. It was neatly placed right on top of all my little papers. God said in his word that he would give seed to the sower. 2nd Corinthians 9:10... I want to brag about God blessing me with two beautiful children because by the way, the doctors said that I couldn't have kids because of the bleeding disorder that I suffered with. I was so sick believe it or not I started believing what they said. The first opportunity that my husband and I had to adopt a baby and we did. As much as we loved our new baby boy I still felt something missing. Yes, I loved him as though I had him but I didn't. God promised us that I would give birth but I allowed discouragement to come and consume me. I repented and said Lord I will believe the report of the Lord. God knows we being in this flesh we mess up sometimes. I thank God for being a forgiving God and a God of another chance. After we got back on track with God he blessed us with a baby girl. After that two years later he blessed us with a baby boy. It is sooooo good to wait on God. Another thing I wanted to brag about God about is my high heels. When I was in the military I used to run five miles a day in these little cheap sneakers. My commander would always tell me Spec. Goddard, you better get some good running sneakers. I said I know but these are so pretty. He said if you don't get sneakers to support your ankles you will regret it in years to come. Well, guess what? I began to suffer from tendonitis in both ankles. You see, sometimes it's good to listen to wisdom no matter where it comes from, God can use anyone. I said Lord, please forgive me. I said Lord please heal my ankles because it hurts so bad. He said ok. He took care of my ankles. You know how sometimes you can have something and don't even realize it. I forgot I asked for-my healing. I used to go shopping and walk right past the heels. One day I said Lord how come I don't wear heels, and he said evidently you don't believe that I healed you. I said Lord I believe you and then I went to the shoe store and bought myself some heels and I have been wearing them ever since. God is sooooo good heels and all.

The Homeless Man Experience

I wanted to share a testimony about a homeless man that I met about a month ago, two of them to be exact. I was shopping for a gift for my husband for Father's Day. Let me go back a little before that. I was cleaning my house and all of a sudden my ears popped wide open. Every time God speaks to me that happens to me. My ears pop open and it seems like I hear waves of water. This happened four times and every time my ears would pop I would say yes Lord speak. I have been doing this for a long time, like forty years long. Every time this happened God always spoke. For some reason, he didn't speak those four times. I said Lord I will be waiting for your voice, still, I heard nothing. Now let me get back to the first homeless guy. When I saw him I told my daughter to slow the car down so I can give him something. When my daughter slowed the car down and blew the horn, the homeless guy walked over to the car. I told him I have something for you and I believe it was ten or twenty dollars I was giving him. He said you have something for me, well I have something for you. I said really, he said yes. He said God has many blessings for you, I smiled and said here you go and I tried to give him the money again. He refused to take the money. He looked me dead in the eyes and said did you hear what I said, I said yes I did. He said do you accept what I said about many blessings are coming to you, I said yes I do. As he was talking to me I was looking into his eyes. The only way I can describe his eyes is they looked as though I was looking into the ocean. He had beautiful blue eyes. The second homeless guy I met was with my husband. I told my husband to stop so we can give him something. When we stopped the car and he came over to the car. You can tell he was drinking. The closer he got the more we smelled him, but that doesn't mean he didn't need help. I told my husband here give him this five dollars. As drunk as he was before he took that money, he said lady you are a blessed woman of God. I looked into his eyes and he had the same eyes as the other guy's ocean blue eyes. We proceeded to go on our way. We were preparing to go to Philadelphia to see my mom who was sick at the time. As my husband and I were driving we ran into a storm on the way to Philadelphia. The storm was so bad that they were telling people to stay in their houses unless you are going to higher ground. We were in the middle of I-95. We could not get out of the car so I just put my head back and closed my eyes. When I opened my eyes I had a vision of Jesus. It was an open vision, I was wide awake. In this vision, I saw Jesus eyes were closed. I thought to myself why are his eyes closed. The first thing I thought was oh he must be sad. All of a sudden he opened his eyes and the same eyes that I saw in the homeless guy I saw in him. I said oh my gosh those eyes again, Jesus without even speaking said the homeless guy you saw that was me. I said wow Lord those eyes, he said yes that was me. You gave it to me. I couldn't get over the eyes of the homeless men so my husband said you sure you didn't entertain an angel. Well, I found out it was not an angel it was the Lord. Matthew 25:31-40. The next time you see someone out there in the streets begging for food or water, don't just walk pass or judge them. You may be walking past the Lord. Jesus said, for I was hungry and you gave me food; I was thirsty and you gave me drink; I was a stranger and you took me in; I was naked and you clothed me; I was sick and you visited me; I was in prison and you came to me. Proverbs 19-17 says whoever is generous to the poor lends to the Lord and he will repay him for his deed. I would like to say God bless you and remember those that are less fortunate than you.

The Health Experience

I would first like to thank God for such a beautiful day this morning. He woke me up and I have the activity of all my limbs. I'm in my right mind and can think on my own. Somebody did not wake up this morning, but I thank God he has given me another day just to say thank you. God has also blessed my husband and me to celebrate thirty-five years of marriage still celebrating. I just wanted to let somebody know never to take their health for granted. Never say oh because I eat all the right food and drink plenty of water and protein, and not to mention exercise every day. That is all good as a matter of fact I need to exercise more and drink plenty of water. God help me I will do better. When I was in the military I did all those things, but some did more than others. I had a first sergeant that was very well trained in taking care of his body eating, drinking, and working out every day. One day we were doing the five-mile run and it seemed as though someone was trying to pull on my foot. Unaware of what was taking place, I felt something of someone pulling on my foot and attempting to free my legs while running, i just kick my legs. All of a sudden our platoon sergeant told us to stop running. I said thank you Jesus because I was tired anyway. Even though everybody was tired we wanted to know why we were told to stop running. We noticed the platoon sergeant running in the opposite direction of where we were going so we followed him. We saw someone lying on the ground. We realized it was the first sergeant. Remember when I said someone was trying to grab my foot, I guess when he was falling he tried to get my attention. He fell down and had a massive heart attack. He died doing what he loved so much. From that day till this day I do not give food or exercise the glory it all belongs to God. That was a very sad day for us. When you get up in the morning say, Lord, I thank you for this day, yesterday is gone and tomorrow I may not see it but God this day I do thank you. Remember someone didn't have a chance to say thank you this morning. Tell the Lord, thank you for my health, someone doesn't have good health today. I remember a time when I could hardly stand up. I was bleeding internally and the doctors didn't know why. I use to lay in my bed saying Jesus if I could only run and give you praise. If I could just raise my arms I would worship. My health was very bad at the time. The doctor even told me that I was going to die because they did everything within their power to do. That was in November 1984. I serve a good God. I remember going to the alter crying with the little strength I had. While I was at the altar I saw a vision of Jesus standing in front of me and he stretched out his robe and handed it to me. By faith, I grabbed his robe and on that day I was totally healed. I no longer say because of what I did I am healthy and whole. All the glory goes to God. Psalms 28:7 says The Lord is my strength and my shield; my heart trusts in him, and he helps me. My heart leaps for joy, and with my song I praise him. He is our strength and our gym. Let's eat more of his word than anything else. And in all things let's give him thanks

The Supernatural Money Manifestation Experience

Well, this is how the story goes, the bible says in Mark 11:23 For verily I say unto you that whosoever shall say unto this mountain, Be thou removed, and be cast sea; and shall not doubt in his heart, but shall believe those things which he saith shall come to pass; he shall whatsoever he saith. That's what the scripture says and I believe it one hundred percent. I believe God and I believe his word, now this is my testimony. I was watching Sid Roth one night. The name of his show is called "It's Supernatural". One night on the show there was a pastor and his wife on the show. The pastor said God told him that he wanted him to go do missions overseas. The place where God wanted him to go would cost him eight thousand dollars. He said Lord all we ever get in the offering is two hundred dollars, God said I didn't ask you what you get I said I need you to go. After church that night God spoke again and said I need you to go on that mission trip. He said okay but we have the same people every week. He said and they have been giving the same every Sunday night. Once again God spoke and said I need you to go overseas, he just knew God did not know what he was talking about. He began to count the money. Every week he received the same offering so he did not expect anything different. He began to count the money. Once he got up to two hundred dollars he knew then that he serves a supernatural God, not a natural God. The Pastor and his wife could not believe that on that night they had received eight thousand dollars. God supernaturally gave them seventy-eight hundred dollars. I was so hyped in my faith after I heard their testimony I said Lord if you did that for them you can do it for me. I said that about two years ago. One night I was taking some money out of a plastic container that I have. My boys and I were taking the dollar bills out to check the serial number to see if the dollars were worth more than a dollar. I knew I had one fifty-dollar bill in the container but everything else was one-dollar bills. I began to pull the money out and one of my boys said here goes a hundred dollar bill. I said no it isn't because I don't have any hundred dollar bills in here. My other son said here goes two fifty dollar bills, I said how can that be because I knew it was only one fifty-dollar bill. All of a sudden I pulled out a stack of brand new twenty-dollar bills. I told the boys y'all count the dollars and I will count the rest of the money. I said Lord what's going on. He said you remembered when you heard the pastor's testimony on how I blessed him supernaturally with his finances, I said yes I remember. He said that's what I did to you. I began to give him praise and honor. I know some may not believe what I am saying but I have the proof. If God can take two fish and five loaves of bread and fed over five thousand surely he can change my dollars from a few hundred to a few thousand. God sent manna from heaven to feed the children of Isreal, when was the last time we got food from heaven? I do believe we shop at Walmart or other grocery stores. We have to know that we serve a supernatural God. The first known miracle in the New Testament is coming from the book of John 2:1-11 when Jesus turned the water into wine. If we would just stand on the word of God and believe it, John 24:12 says in the KJV Verily verily I say unto you, He that believeth on me, the works that I do shall he do also; and greater works than these shall he do; because I go to my father. Hebrews 11:1-2 says Now faith is the substance of things hoped for, the evidence of things not seen. For by it the elders obtained a good report. Come on, where is your report? Not only should the elders have a good report, so should we.

Conclusion

I finally shared a few of my testimonies that God has allowed me to experience. I am more in love with God more today than yesterday. I will continue to walk in the supernatural power of God with boldness and authority. I also pray that you began to experience God in a whole new way. Come on let's do the work that Jesus did plus more. Let signs and wonders follow us and not us following signs and wonders.

CPSIA information can be obtained
at www.ICGtesting.com
Printed in the USA
BVHW032304250922
647977BV00015B/347

9 781662 850318